STAINED GLASS PATTERN BOOK

STAINED GLASS PATTERN BOOK

MARIA DI SPIRITO

Sterling Publishing Co., Inc.
New York

Library of Congress Cataloging-in-Publication Data Available

10   9   8   7   6   5   4   3

Published in 2003 by Sterling Publishing Co., Inc.
387 Park Avenue South, New York, NY 10016
Originally published in Italy by Il Castello–Collane
Tecniche–Milano–S.r.l.
V.C. Ravizza 16, Milan, 20149
under the following titles:
45 Vetrate © 1992 Il Castello
45 Vetrate a motivi floreali © 1994 Il Castello
45 Vetrate a motivi geometrici e astratti © 1995 Il Castello
45 Vetrate per porte © 1999 Il Castello
Distributed in Canada by Sterling Publishing
c/o Canadian Manda Group
One Atlantic Avenue, Suite 105
Toronto, Ontario, M6K 3E7, Canada
Distributed in Great Britain by Chrysalis Books
64 Brewery Road, London, N7 9NT, England
Distributed in Australia by Capricorn Link (Australia) Pty. Ltd.
P.O. Box 704, Windsor, NSW 2756, Australia

Sterling ISBN 1-4027-0269-8

CONTENTS

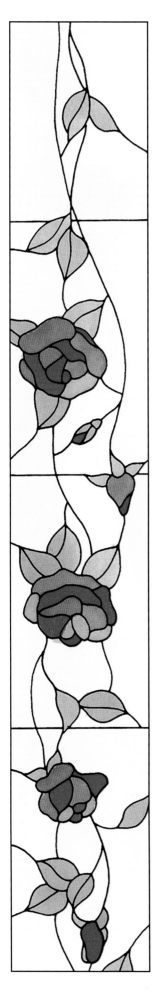

INTRODUCTION

It is said that the history of glass begins with Pliny (A.D. 23-79), a Roman writer of natural history, whose tale describes the accidental discovery of glass by Phoenician sailors who placed their cooking pots on blocks of natron (soda) over fires they had built on the beach. The next morning, the fire's heat had melted the sand and soda mixture, dried, and then hardened into glass. Unfortunately, this legend has not been scientifically proven. It is believed that Egyptian or Mesopotamian potters most likely discovered glass by accident when firing their vessels. Egyptian beads that date from 2750 to 2625 B.C. are the earliest manmade glass. The Romans used blown glass for domestic uses such as goblets, vases, and drinking glasses.

The first recorded production of glass sheets dates from the 1st century by the Romans who had mastered the blown glass technique and made thin, transparent sheets which they used for window panes. Due to their high cost, they were only placed in public buildings. Not until the Middle Ages were glass sheets assembled with lead came, thus creating the first artistic stained glass panels. Stained glass flourished in the cathedrals throughout Europe. Religious figures were the most popular subjects and the predominant colors were blue, red, yellow, and green. As larger church walls were built, a greater variety of stained glass became common like Gothic rose windows in the 13th century. A wider range of purples, dark greens, and yellows were also added to the color palette.

After some time, the stained glass technique began to deteriorate once artists learned how to color glass by painting enamel over clear glass. Instead of using lead came, artists in the 17th and 18th centuries began to paint lead lines with enamel, which made the lead lines loose their artistic meaning. This new technique allowed for all church windows to be made with just ordinary colored glass.

In the 19th century stained glass made its comeback with the help of two innovative American painters who began to experiment with glass, John LaFarge and Louis Comfort Tiffany. They soon became competitors as they both searched for glass that possessed a wide range of effects. LaFarge developed and copyrighted opalescent glass in 1879. It differed from other glasses in that several colors were combined and manipulated to create a wide range of hues and three-dimensional effects. Soon after

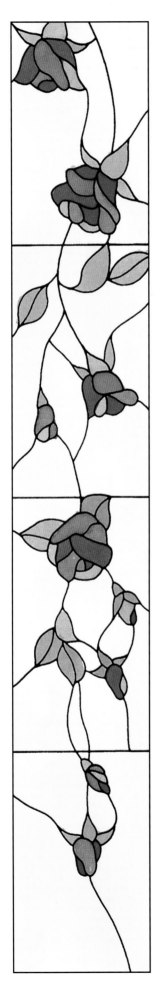

Tiffany also registered for a patent. Both Tiffany and LaFarge used intricate cuts and richly colored glass in detailed designs. By using thin strips of copper lead, instead of lead came, they were able to create intricate sections within widows for both churches and private homes. Tiffany then adapted the technique to make lampshades for electrical lighting, which had just been invented. He was an instant success. Many Tiffany technique imitators soon were everywhere and opalescent windows and shades remained popular throughout the century. Even today, his name is synonymous with lampshades.

The stained glass designs in this book can all be used with any of the stained glass techniques: Tiffany, traditional, collage, mock, and grisaille. They can also be used in a variety of ways: Lampshades, table tops, decorative boxes, folding screens, mirrors, windows, and panels are only but a few examples. Photocopy the design. (Remember; you can always reduce or enlarge the copy in order to meet your needs.) The colors we use are only suggestions. Be creative and come up with your own color schemes! We have broken the book into four sections. In Section 1 we focus only on beautiful floral patterns. In Section 2 we copied designs that nature alone could create. Section 3 focuses on stained glass panels for doors, mirrors, room dividers, or table tops. Section 4 specializes in modern geometrical patterns that were inspired by Frank Lloyd Wright.

Now then, enough talking. It's time to get to work. I hope you enjoy the designs, and I wish you the best of luck with your projects!

Maria di Spirito

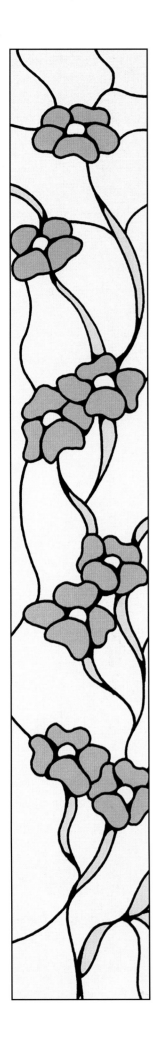

SECTION 1

FLORAL PATTERNS

13

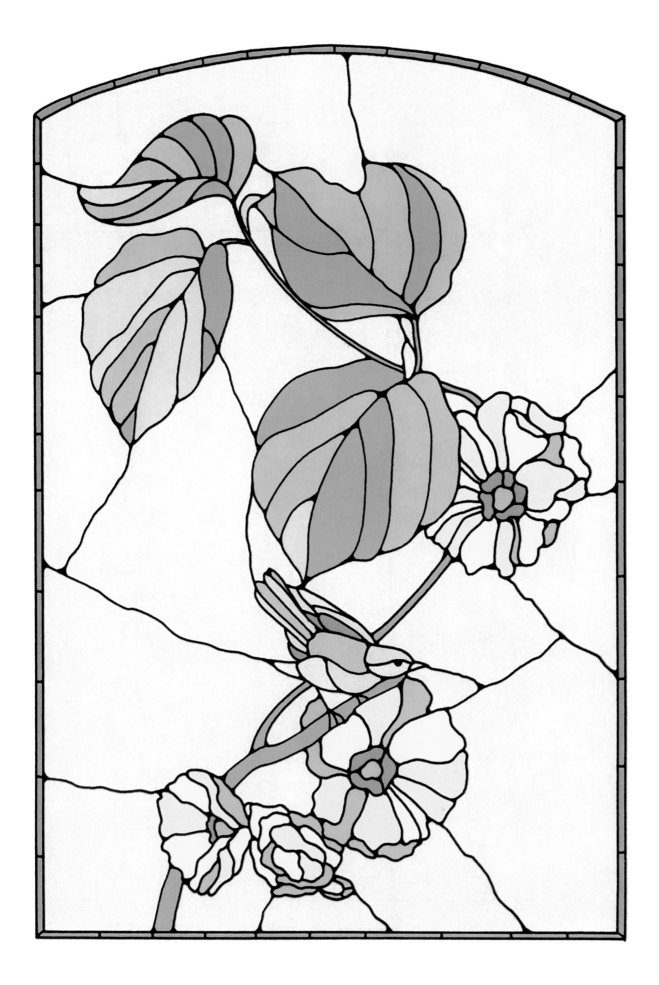

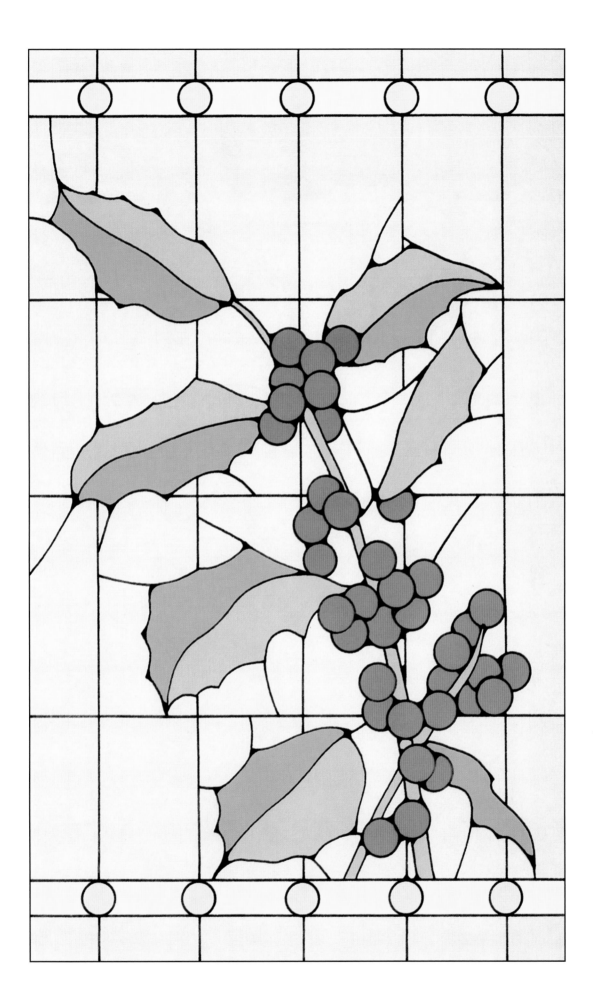

19

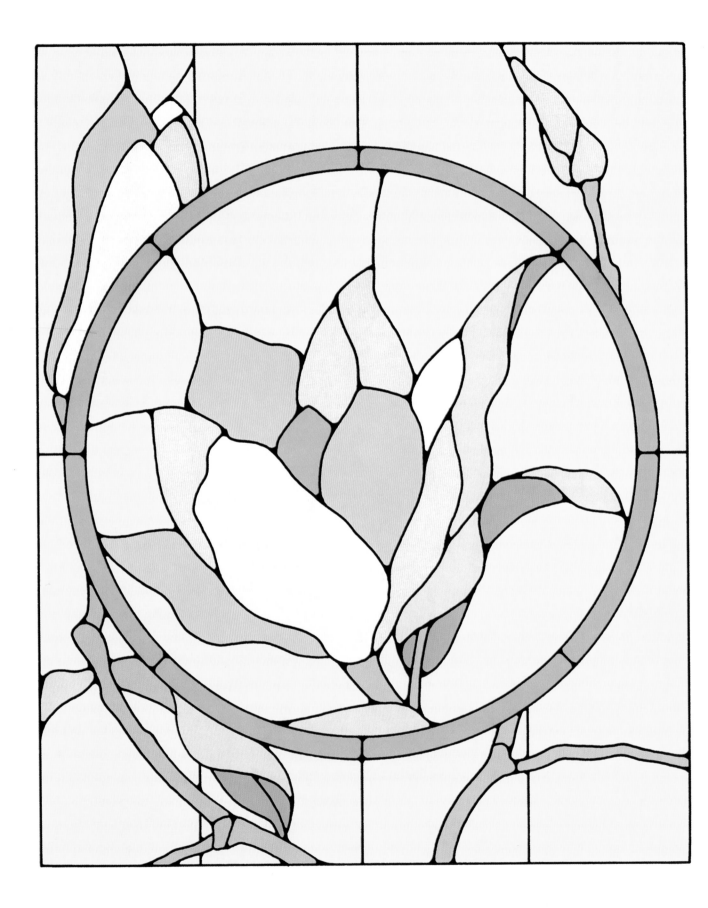

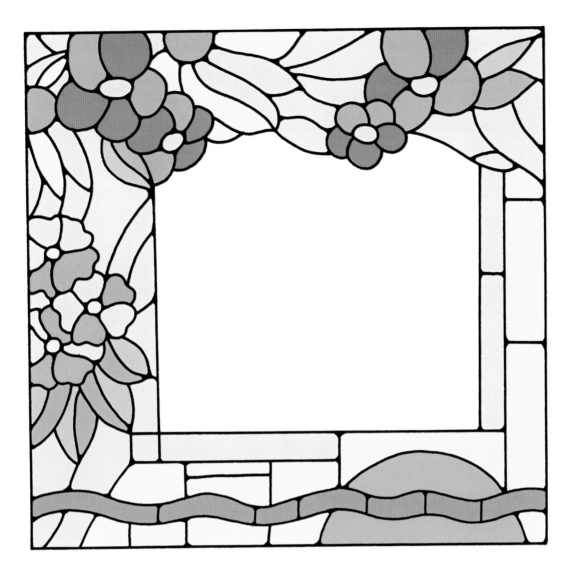

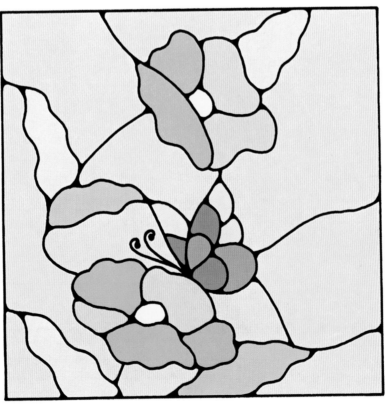

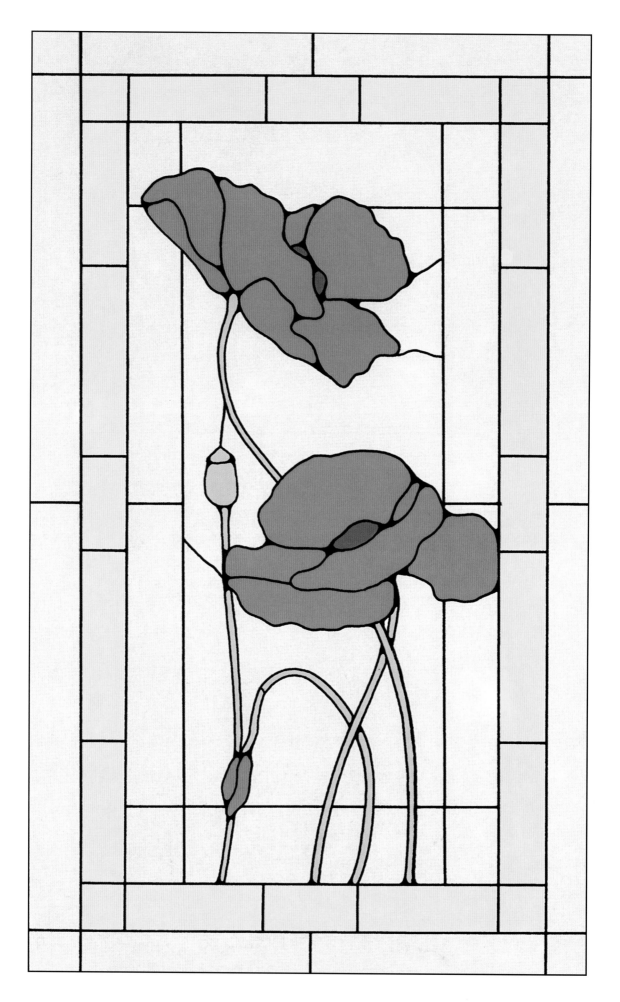

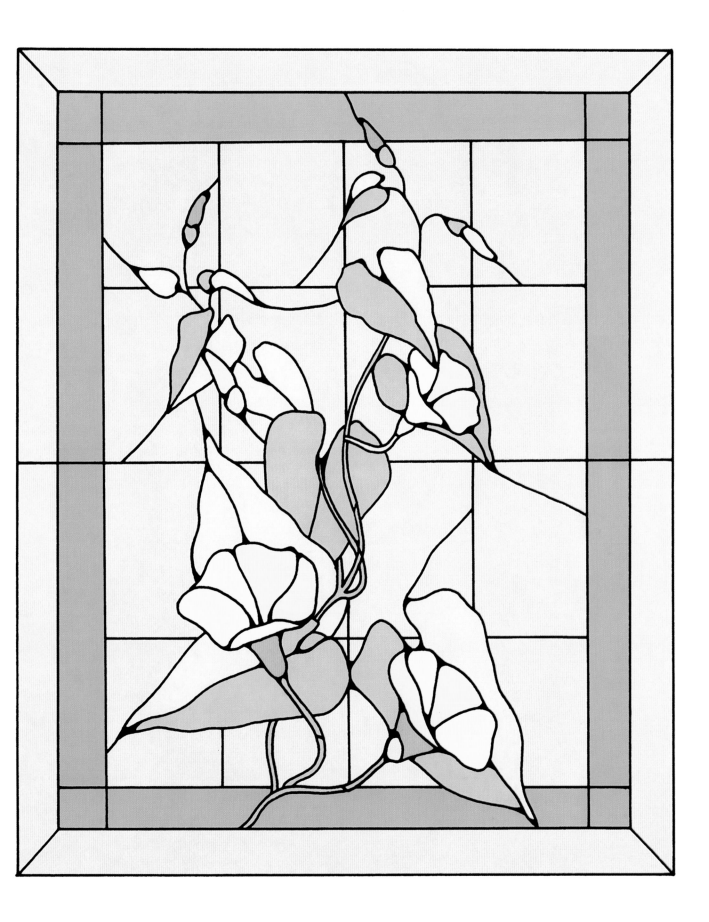

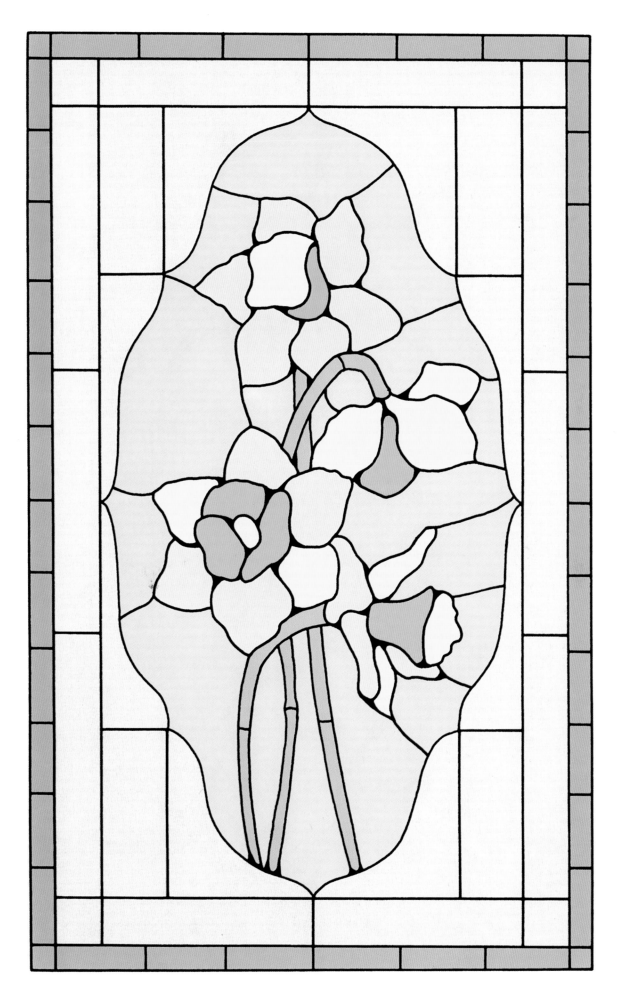

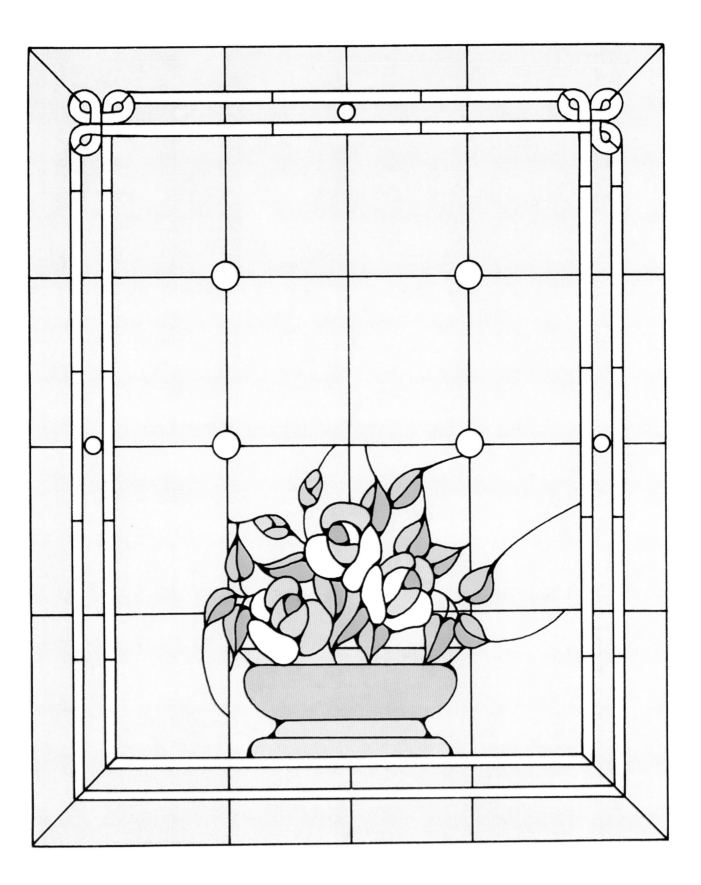

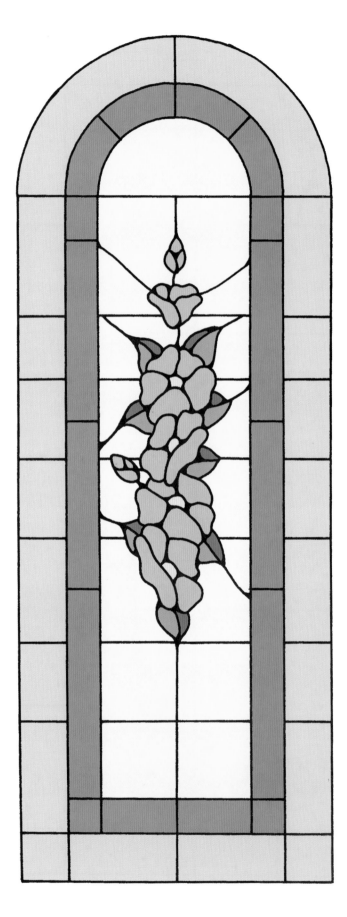

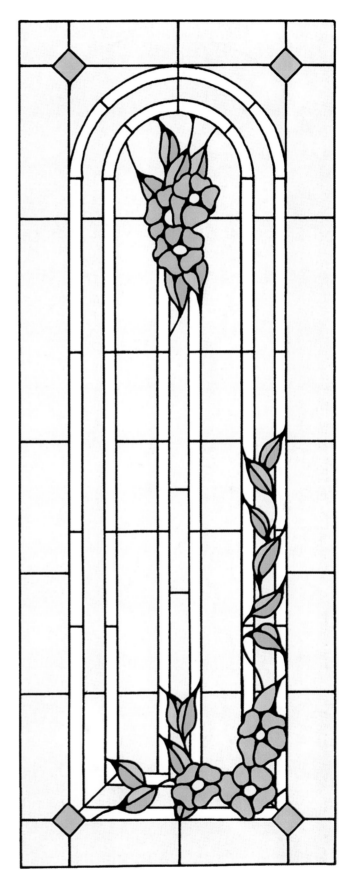

35

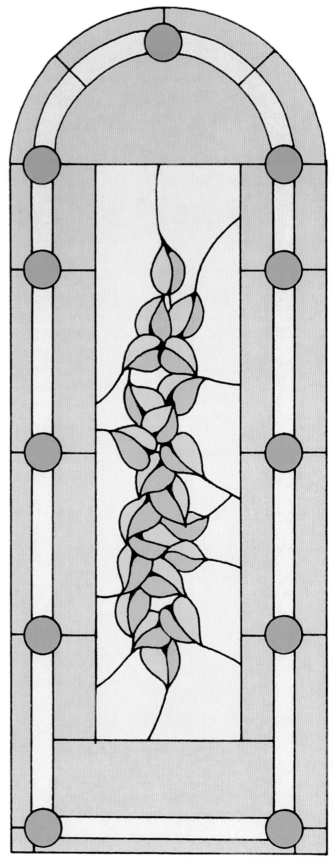

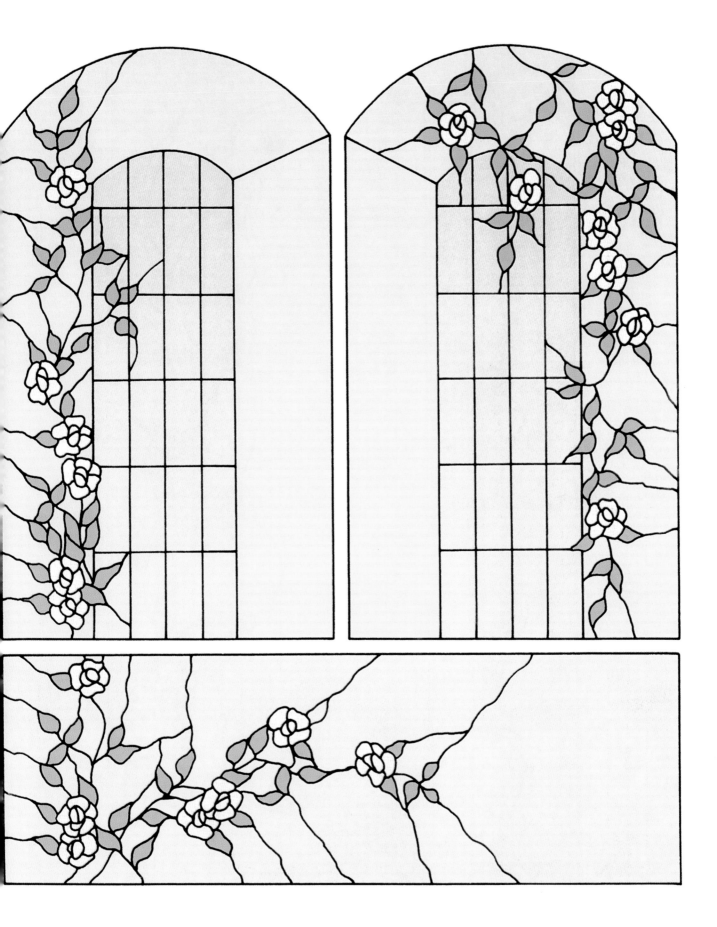

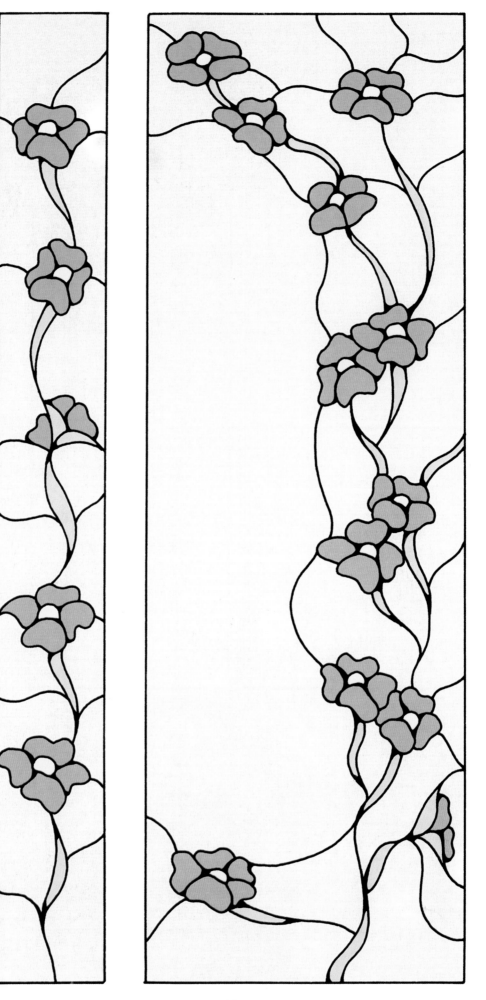

38

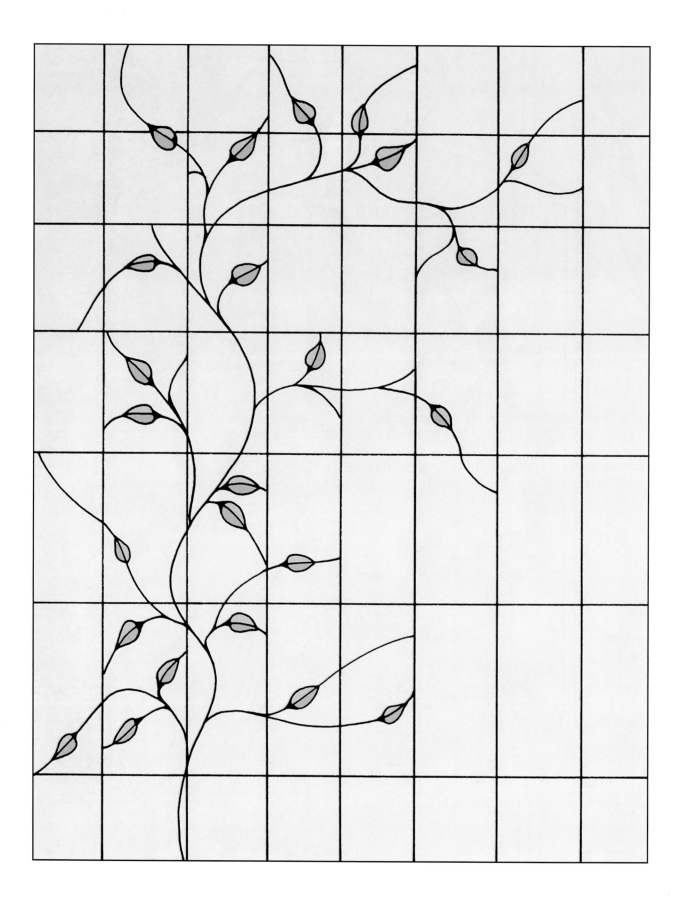

40

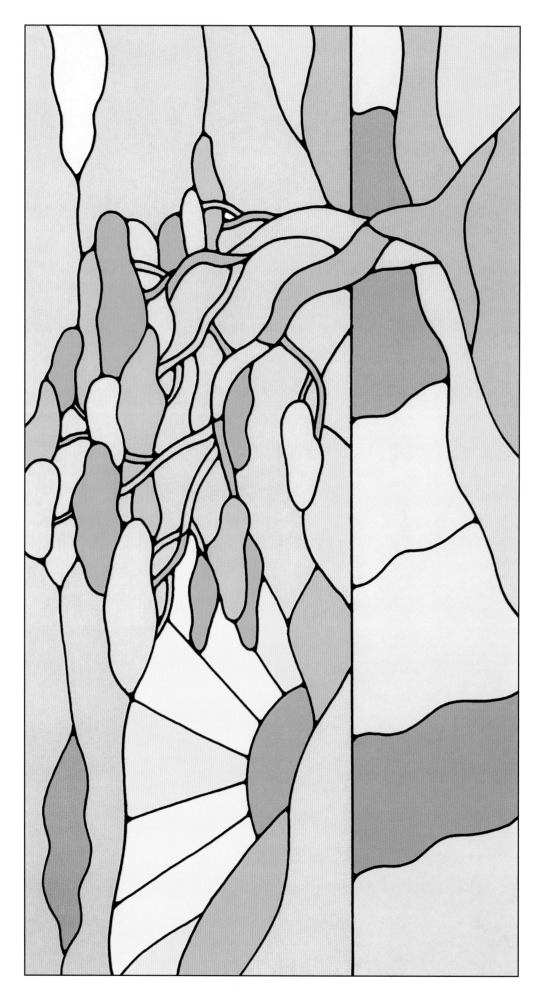

44

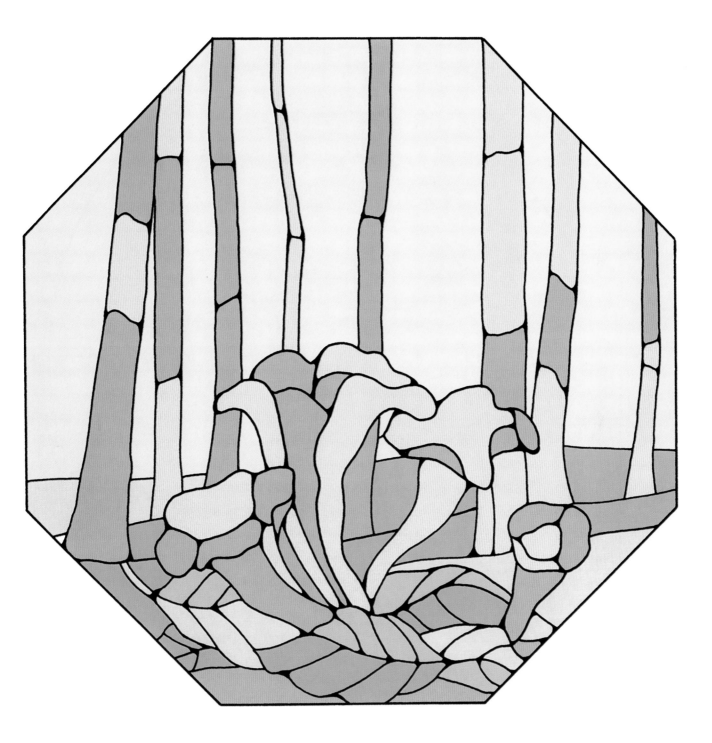

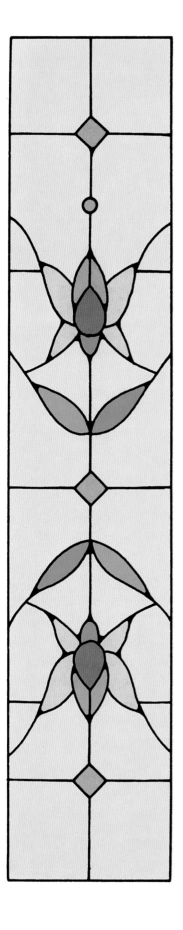

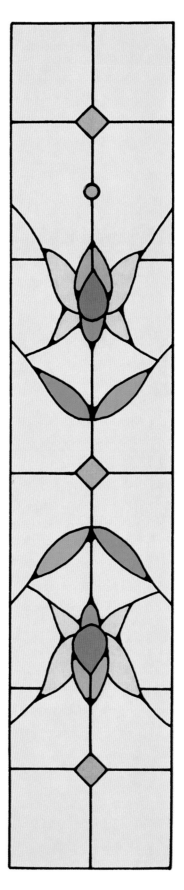

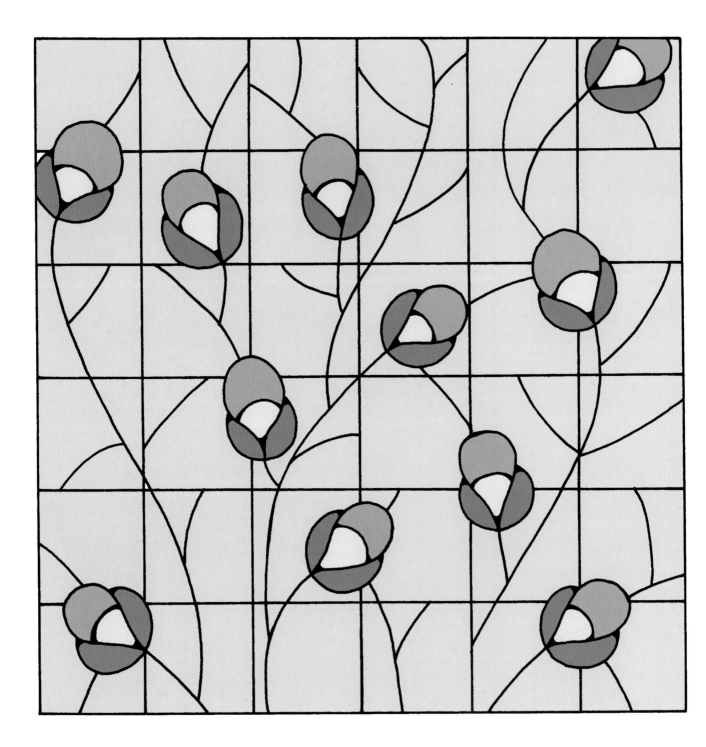

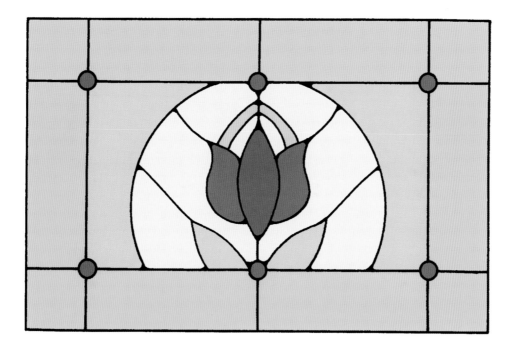

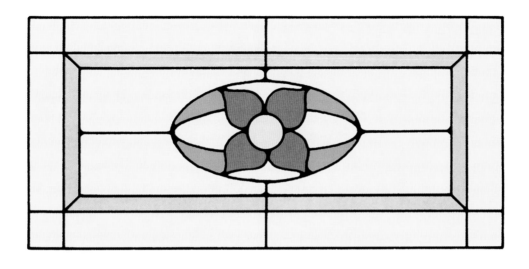

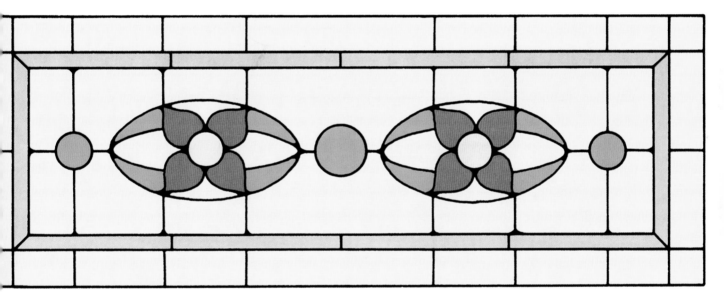

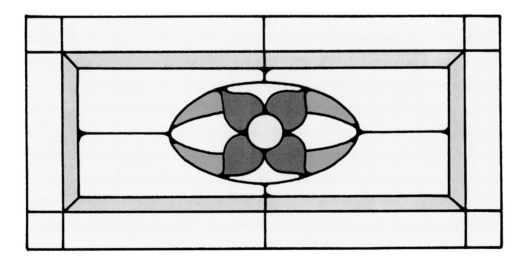

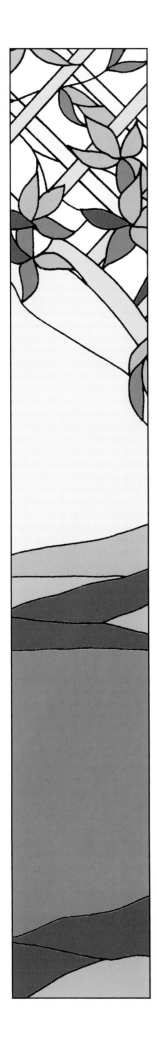

SECTION 2

NATURE PATTERNS

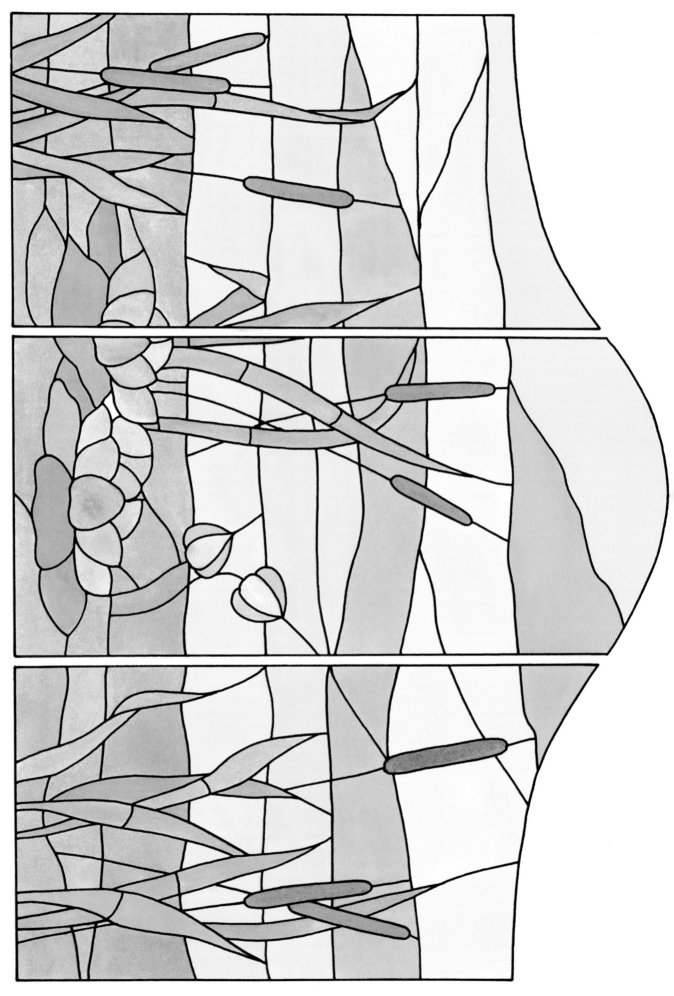

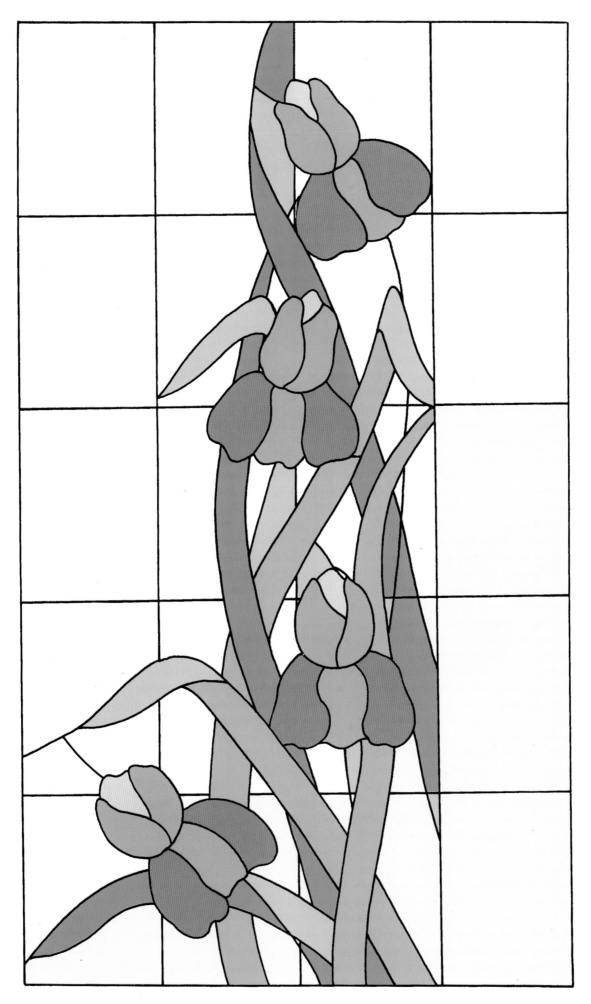

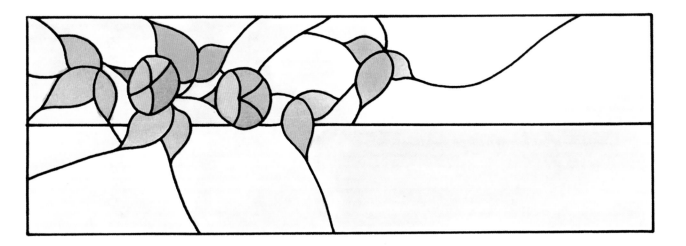

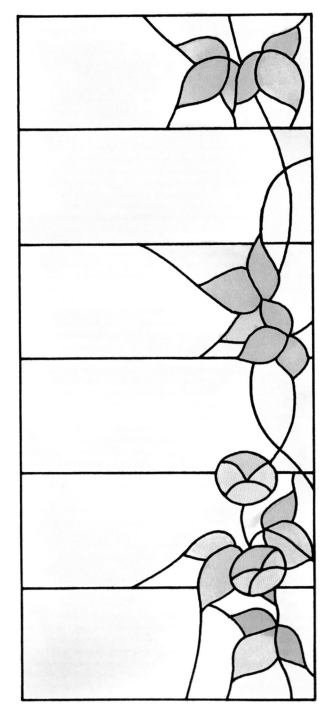

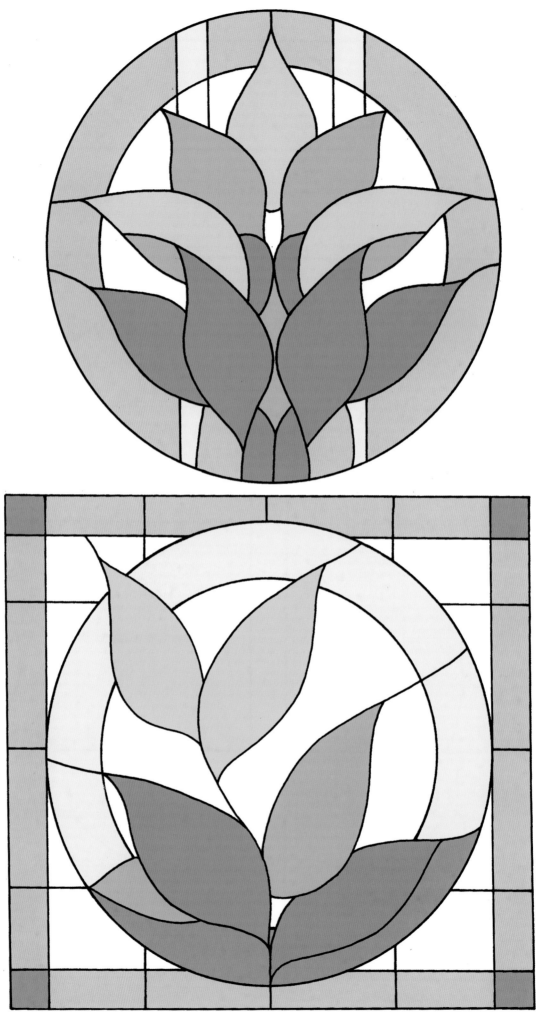

70

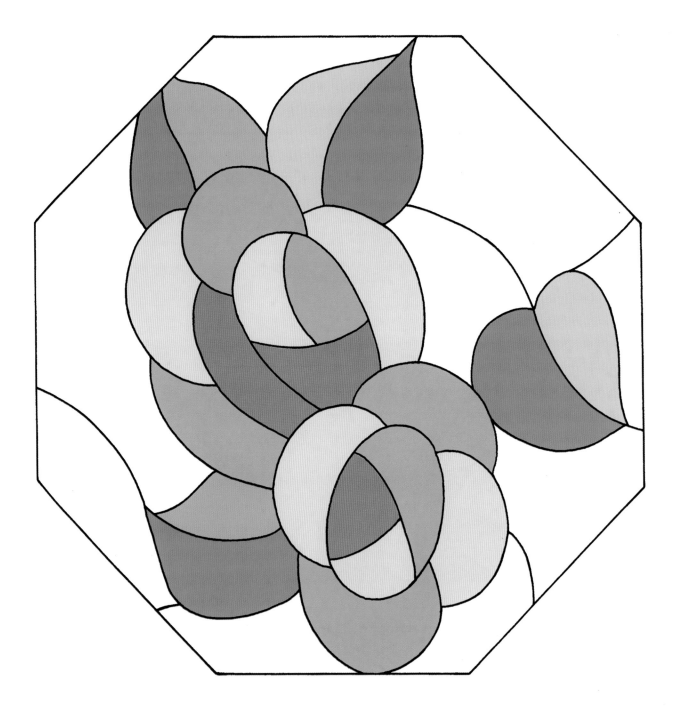

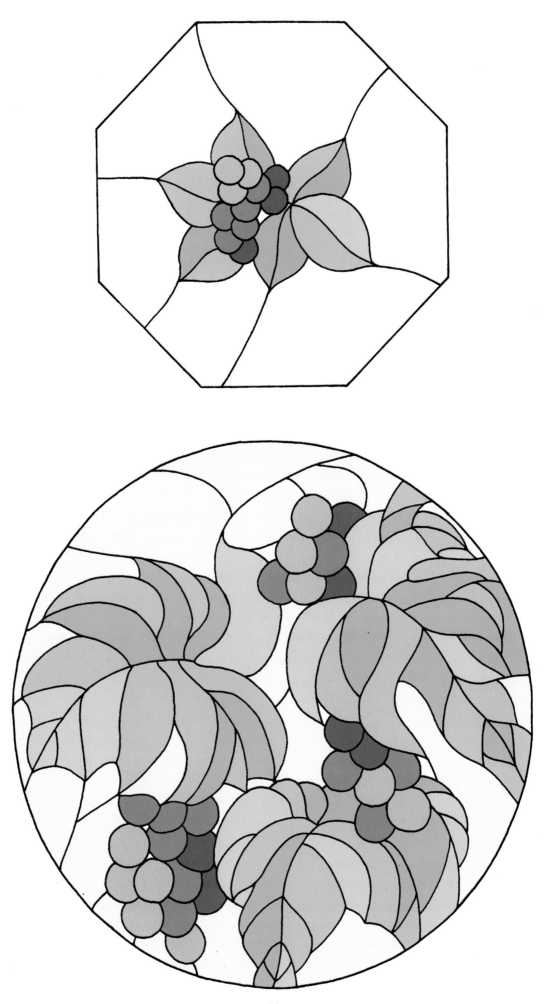

80

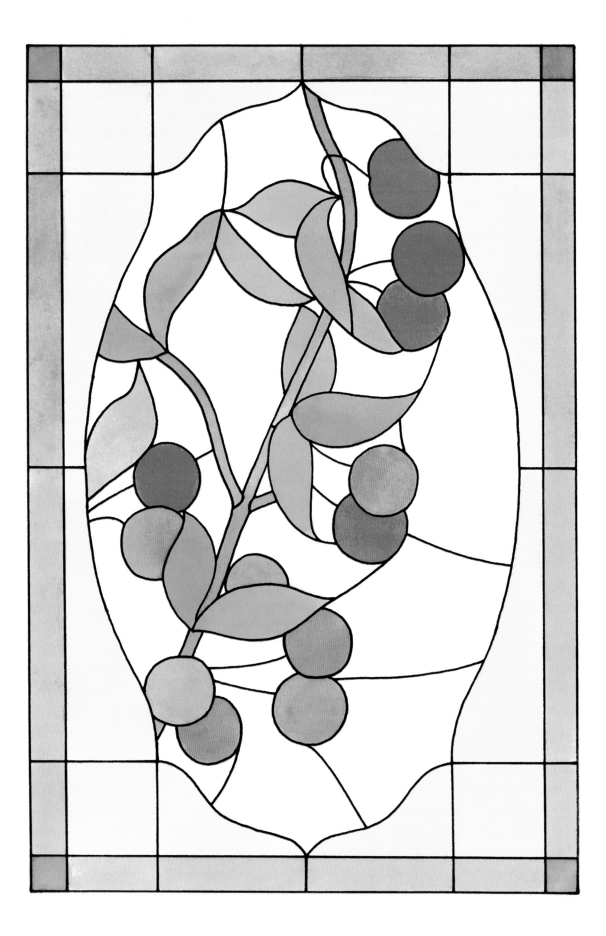

81

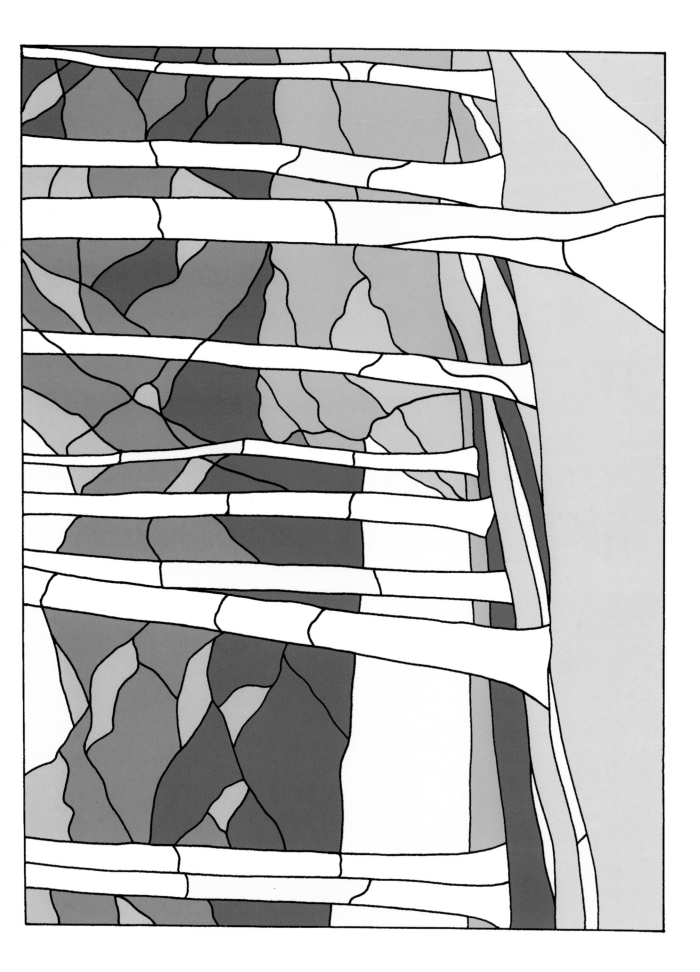

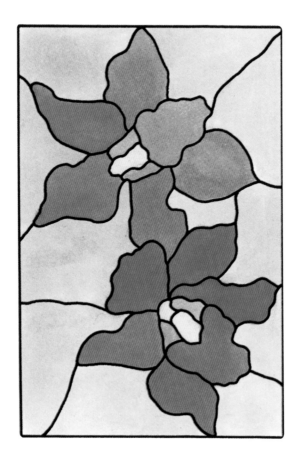

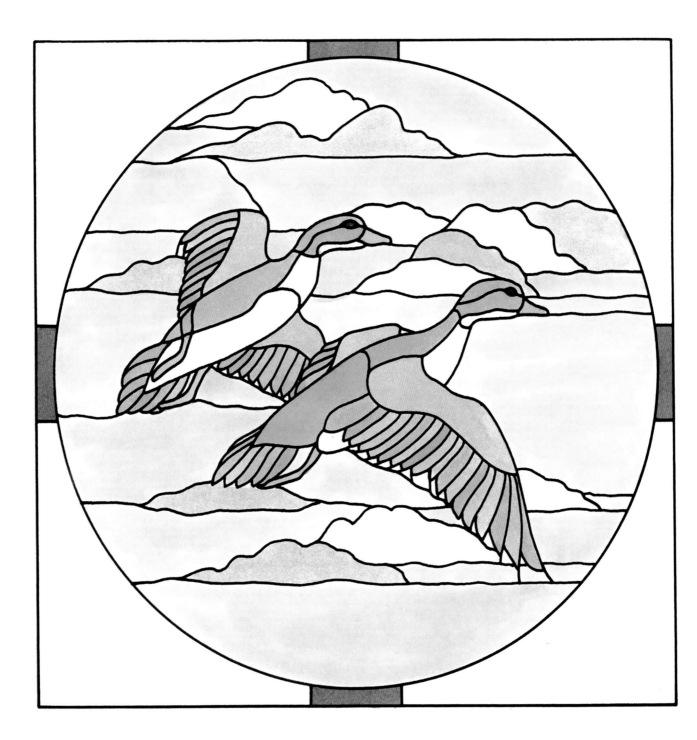

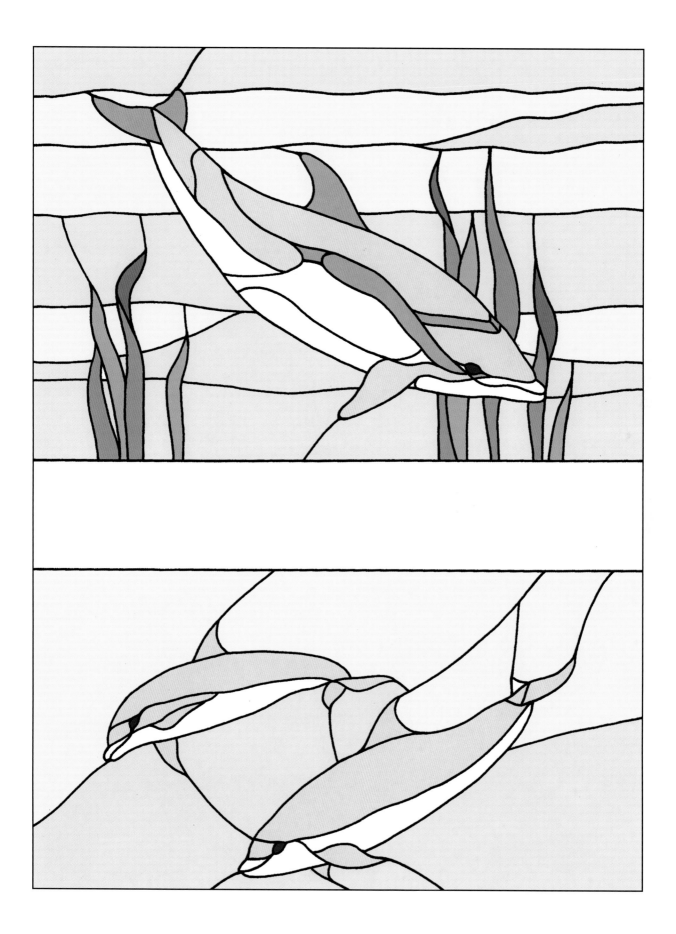

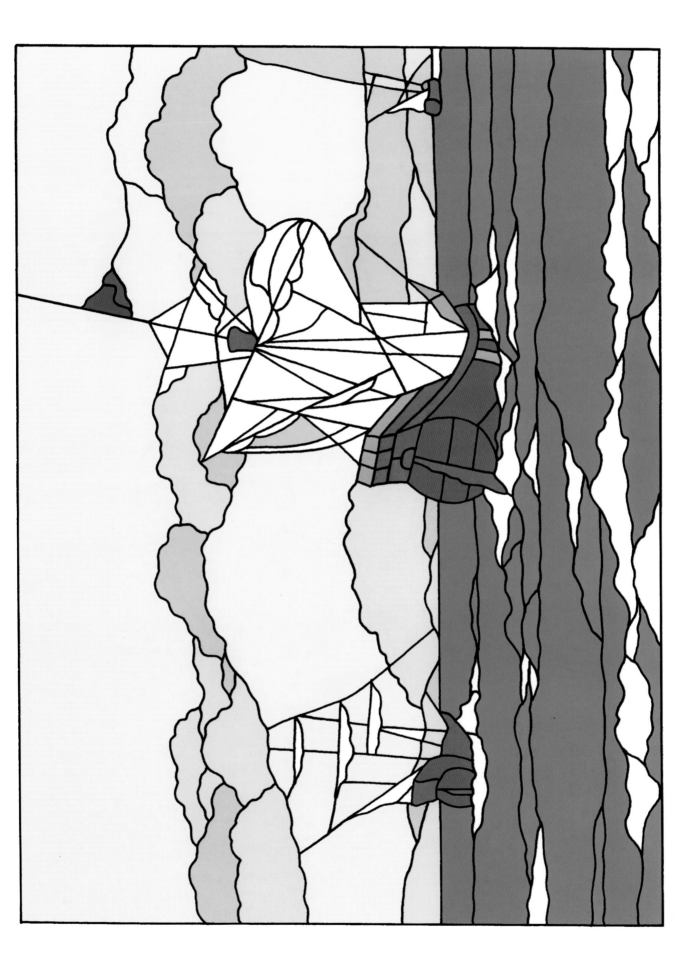

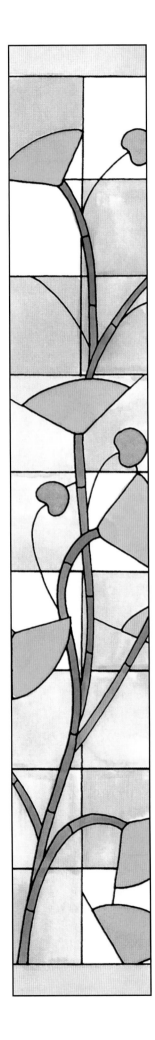

SECTION 3

PANEL PATTERNS

106

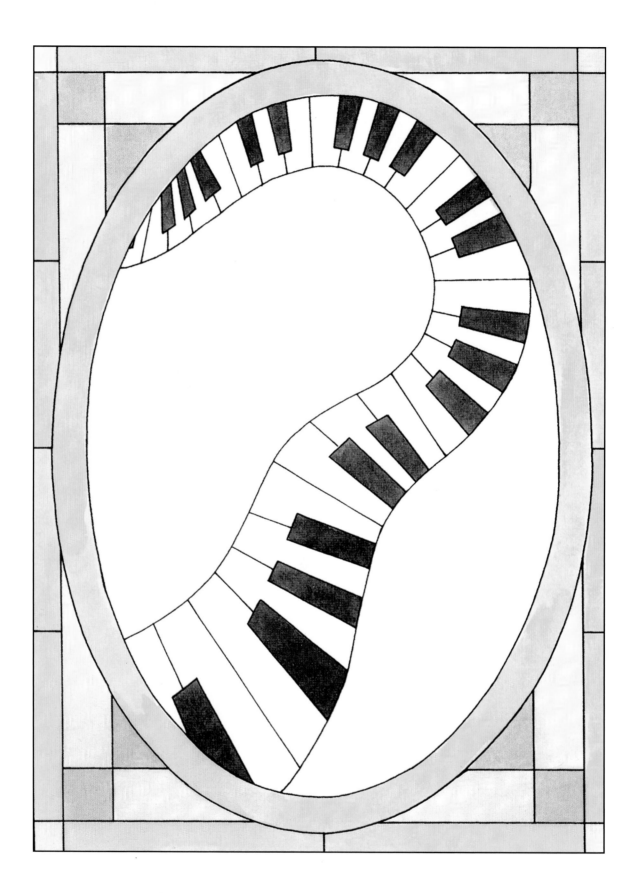

A

B

B

A

113

114

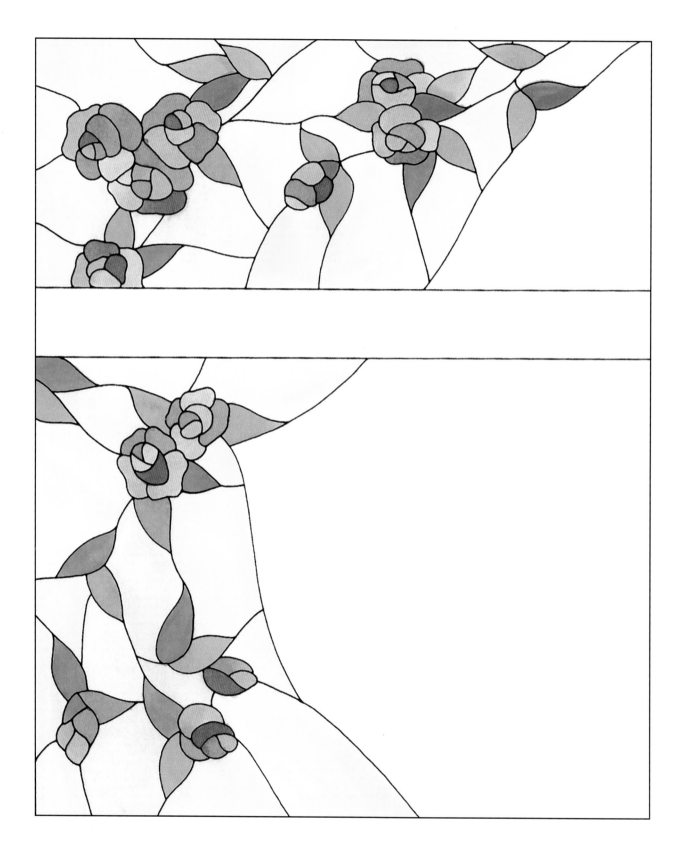

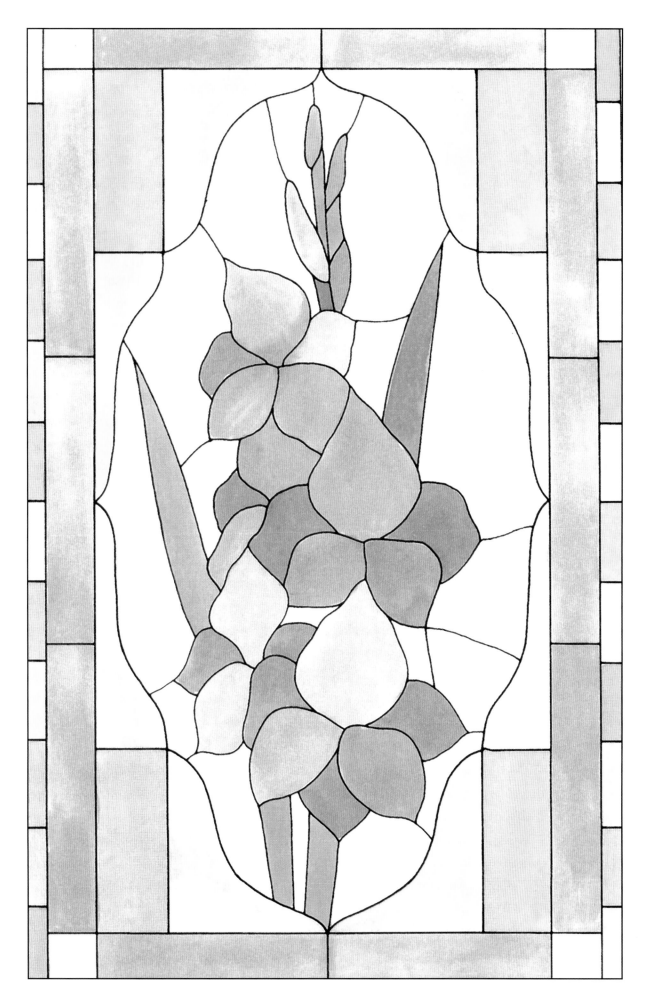

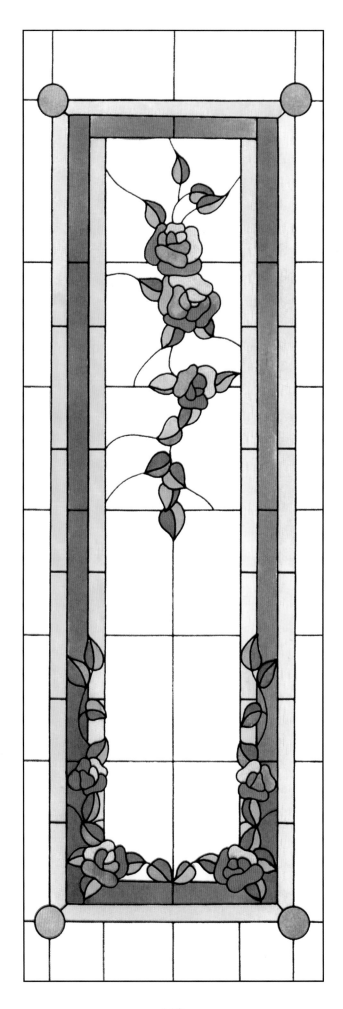

121

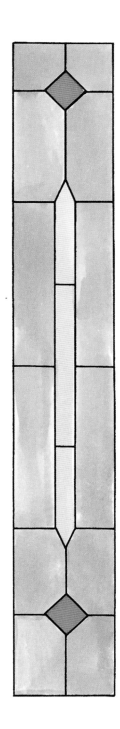

127

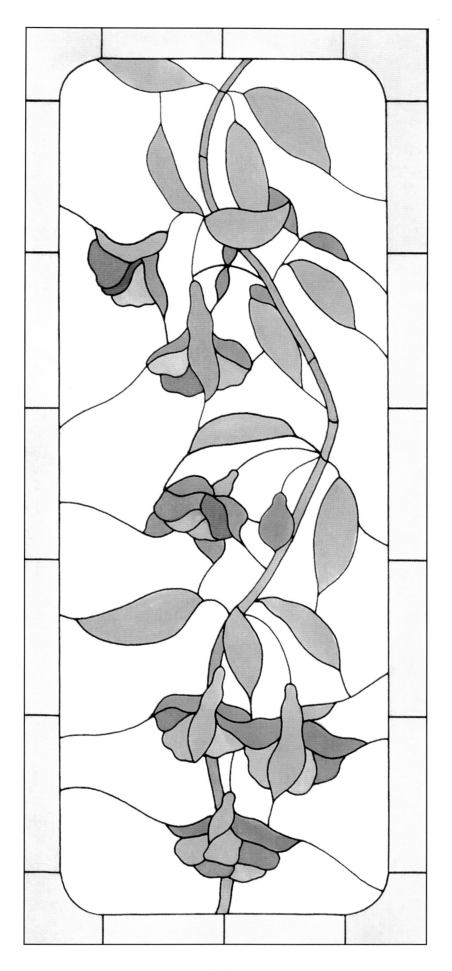

133

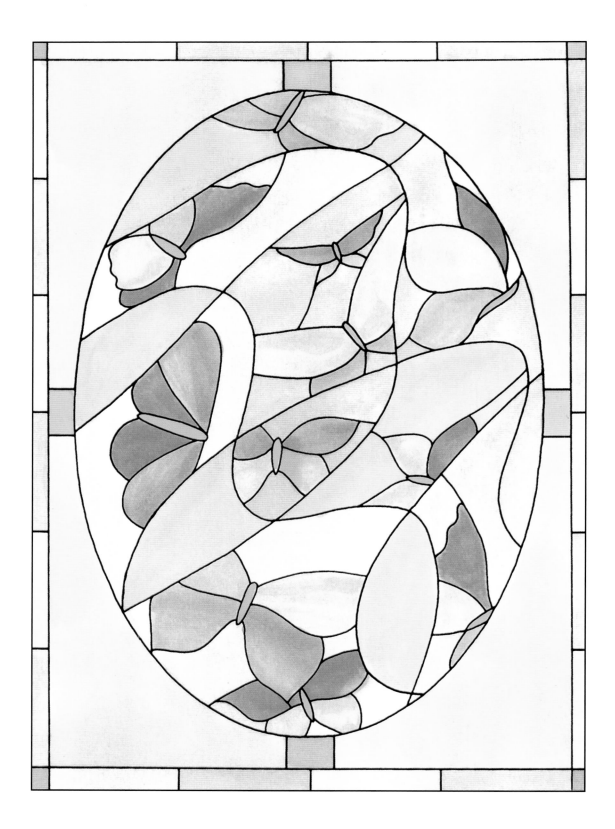

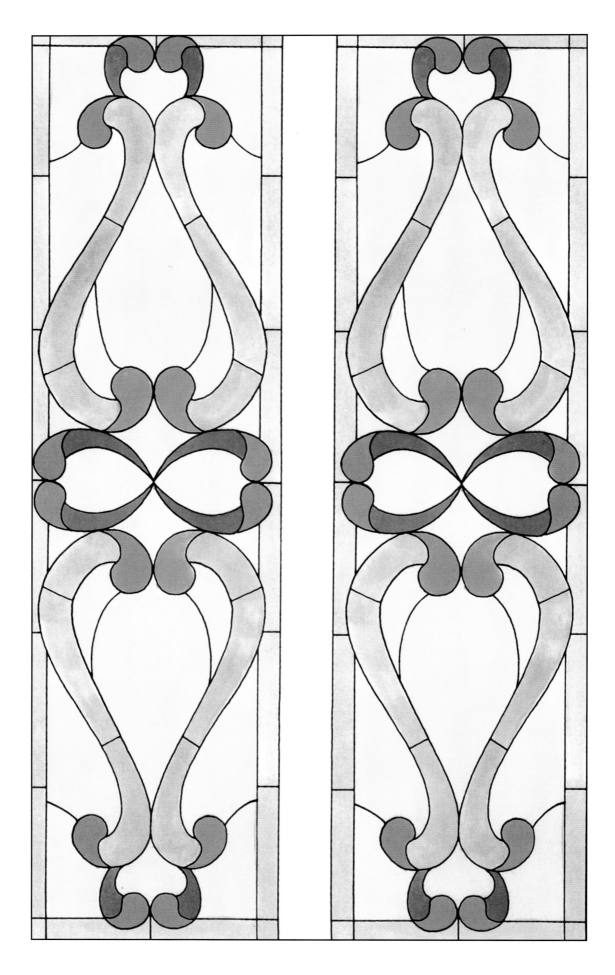

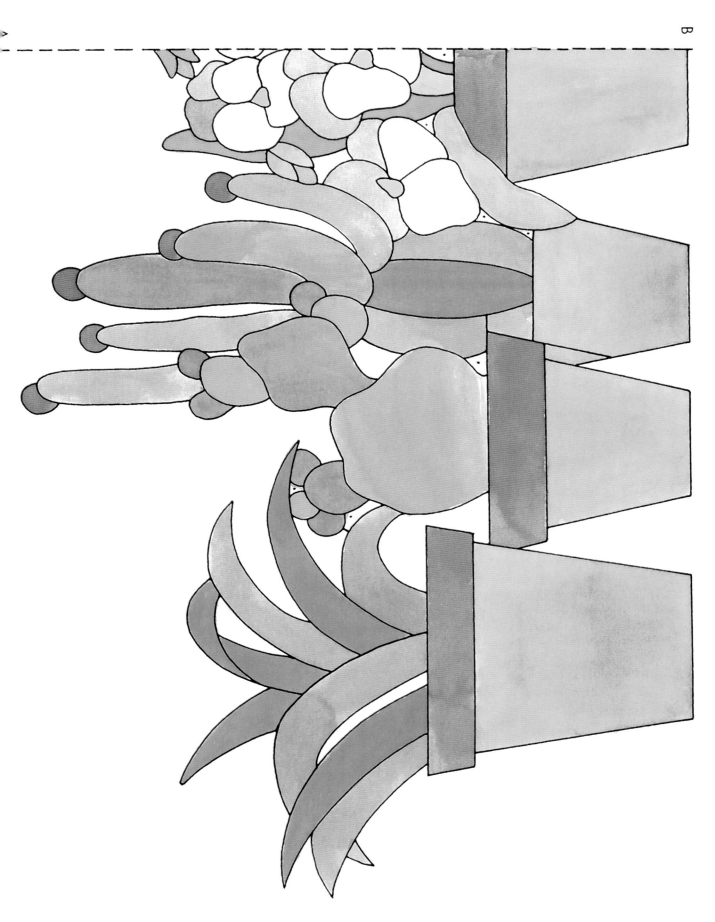

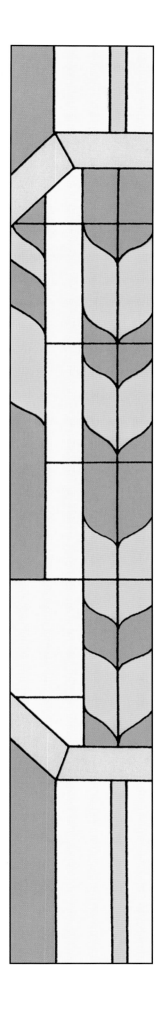

SECTION 4

GEOMETRICAL PATTERNS

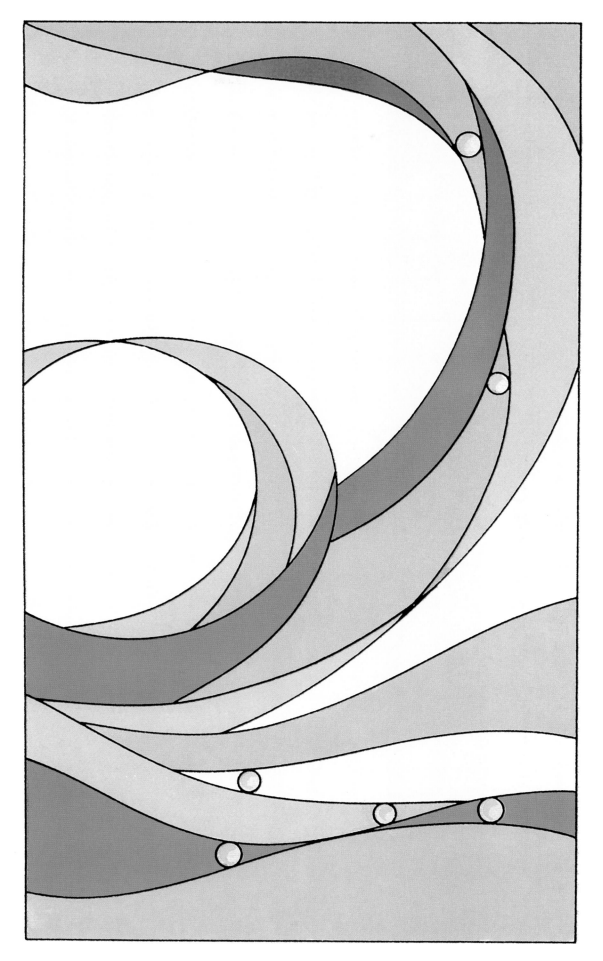

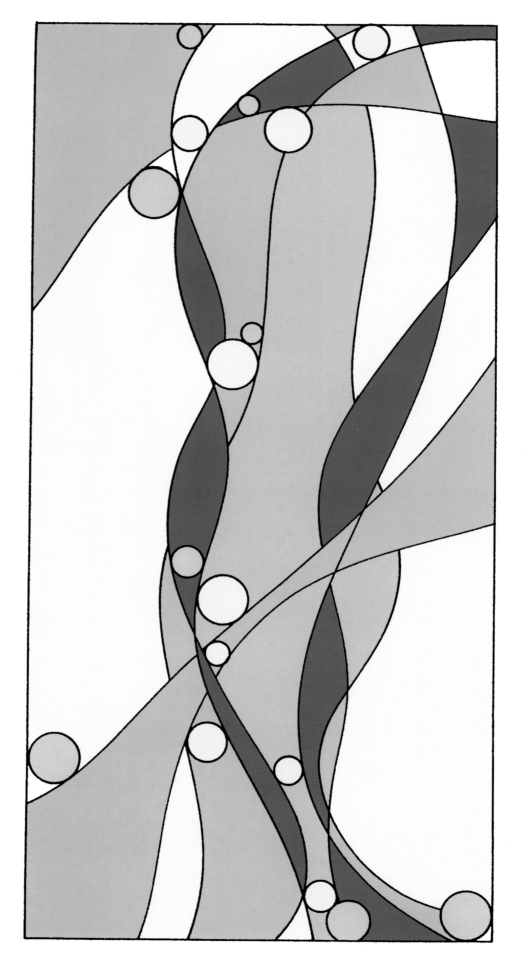

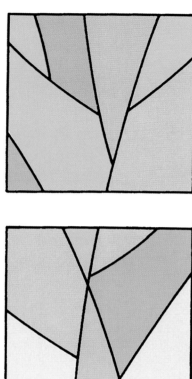

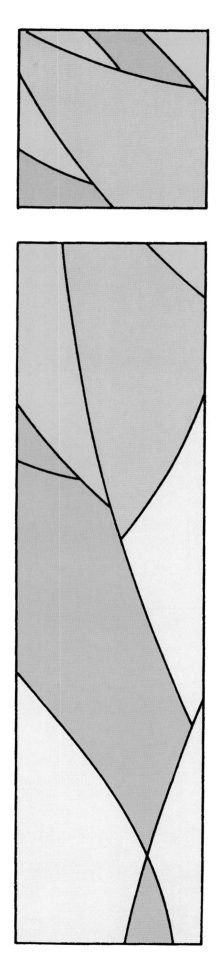

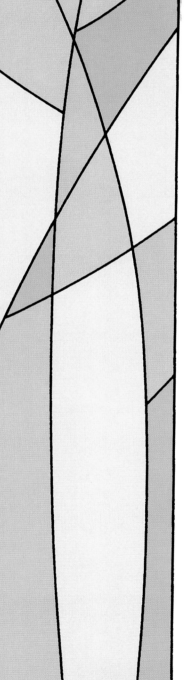

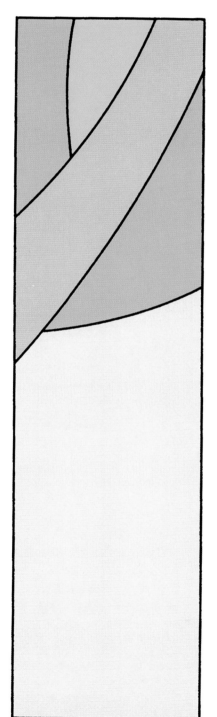

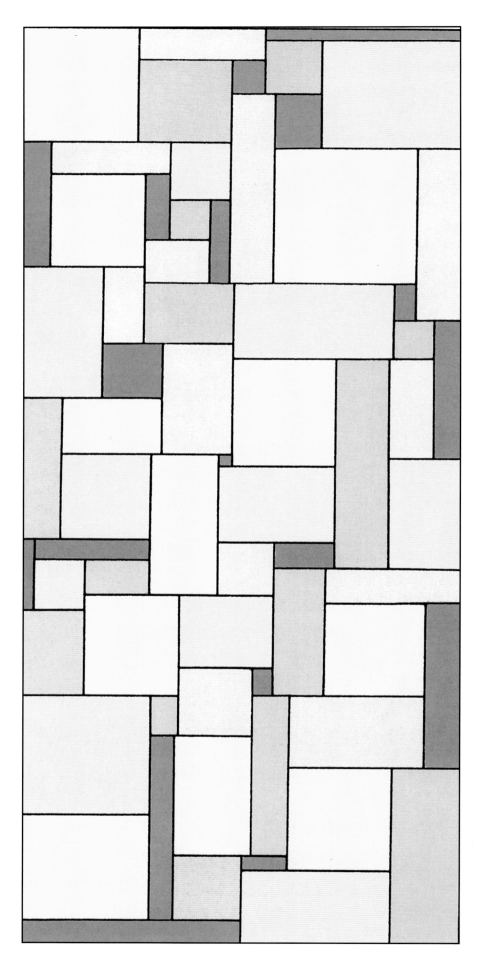

154

156

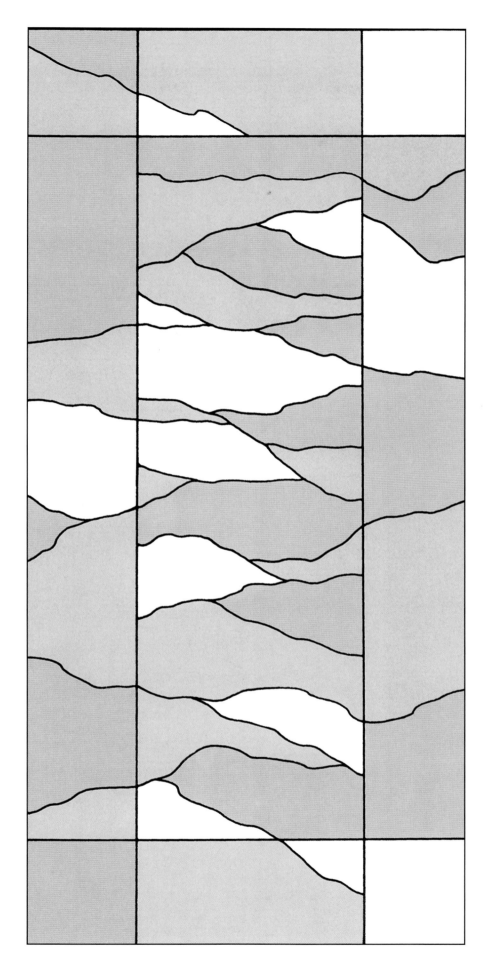

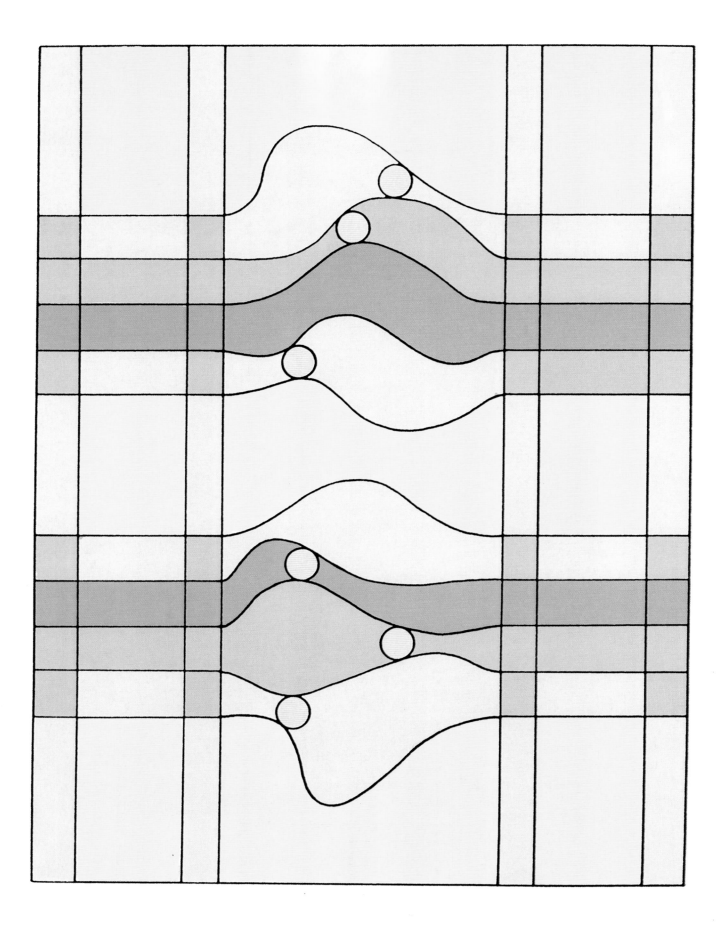

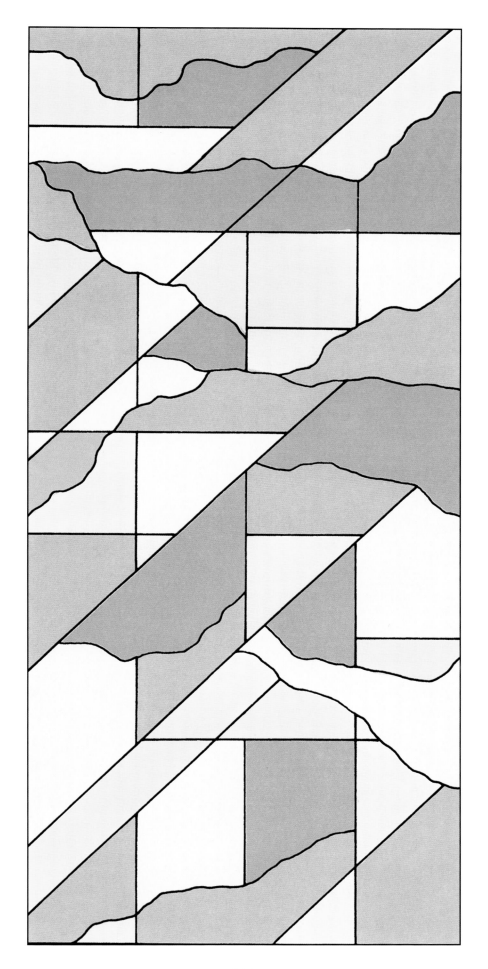

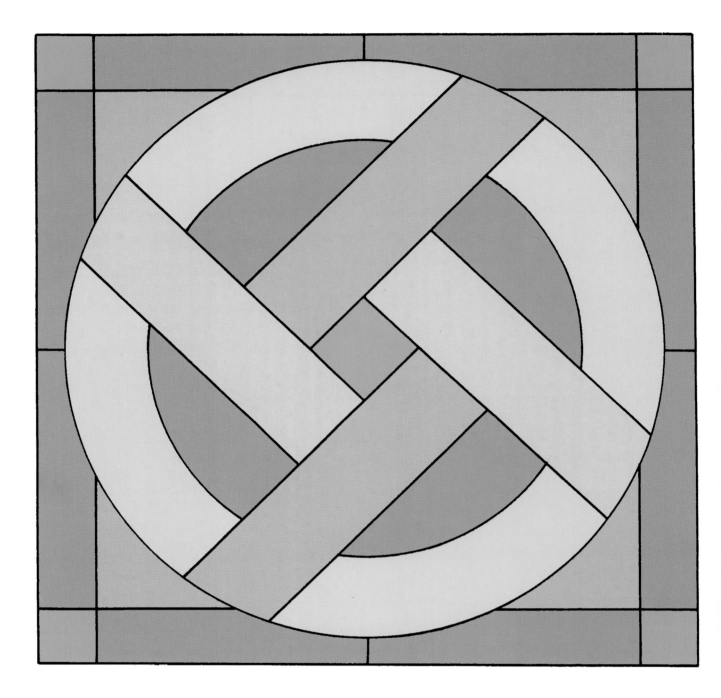

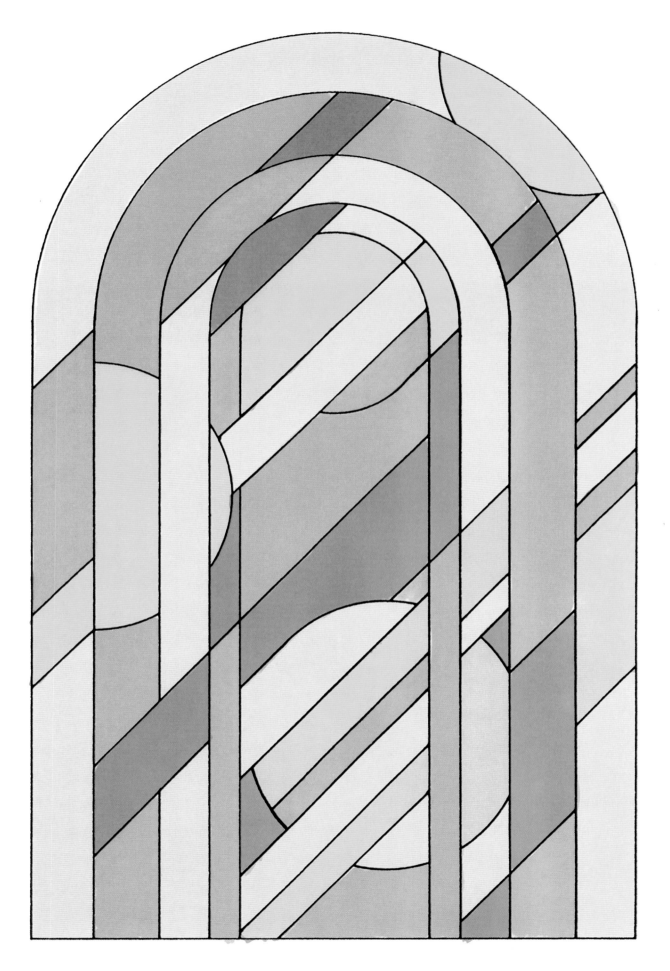

164

165

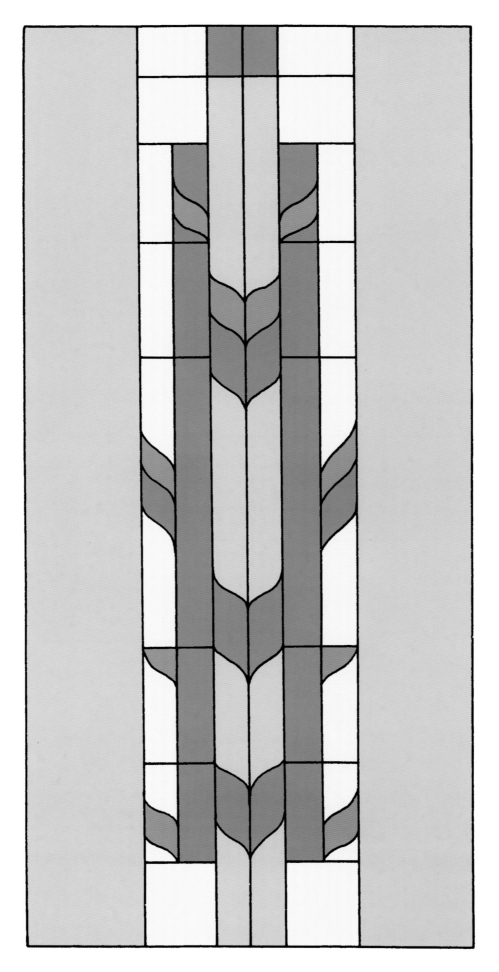

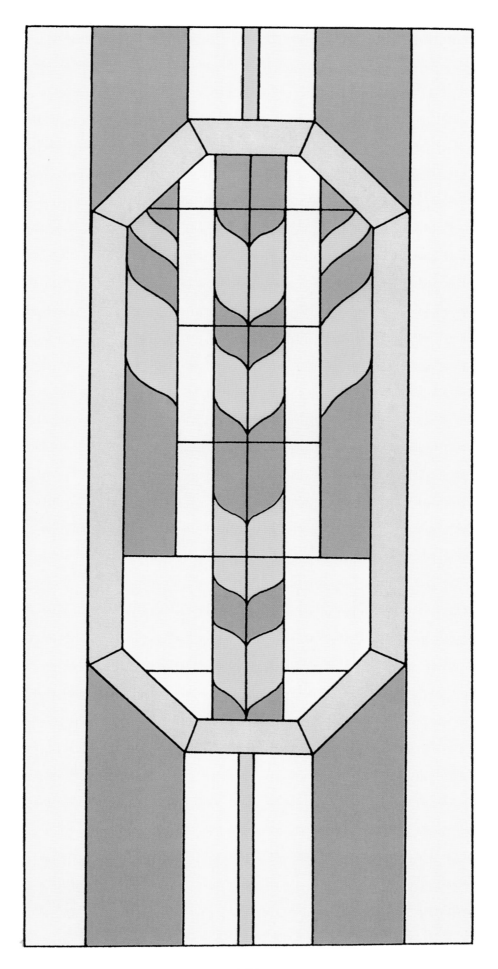

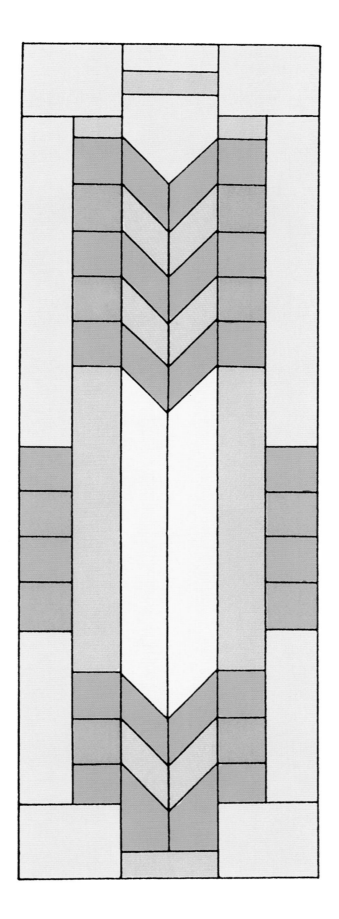

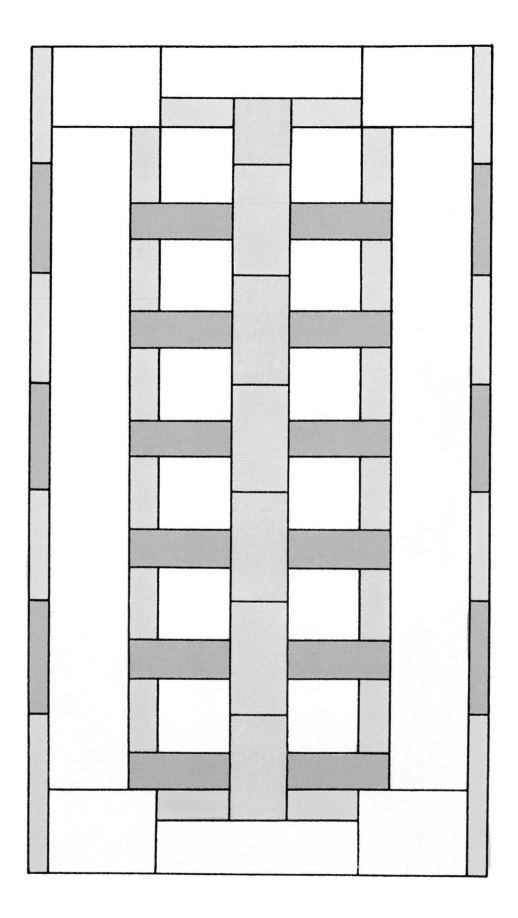

172

173

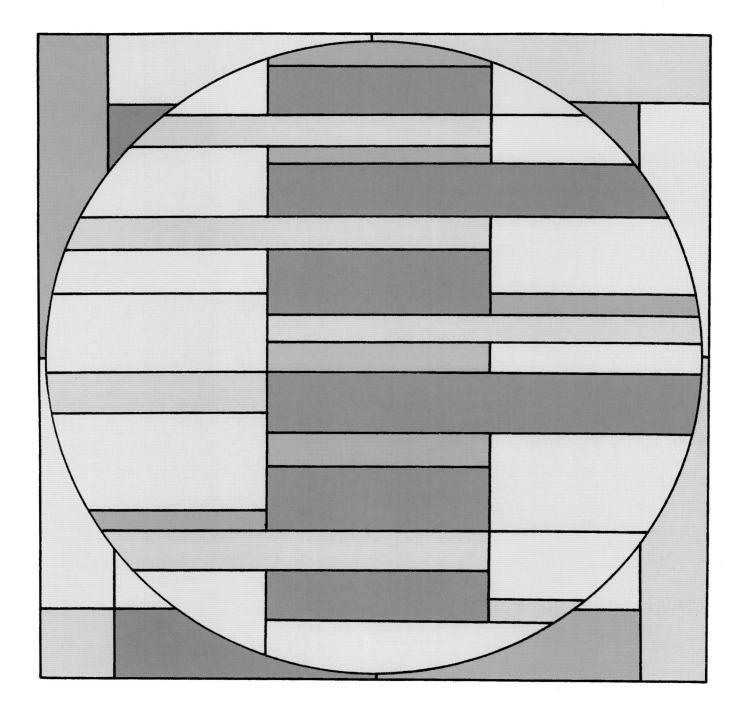

176

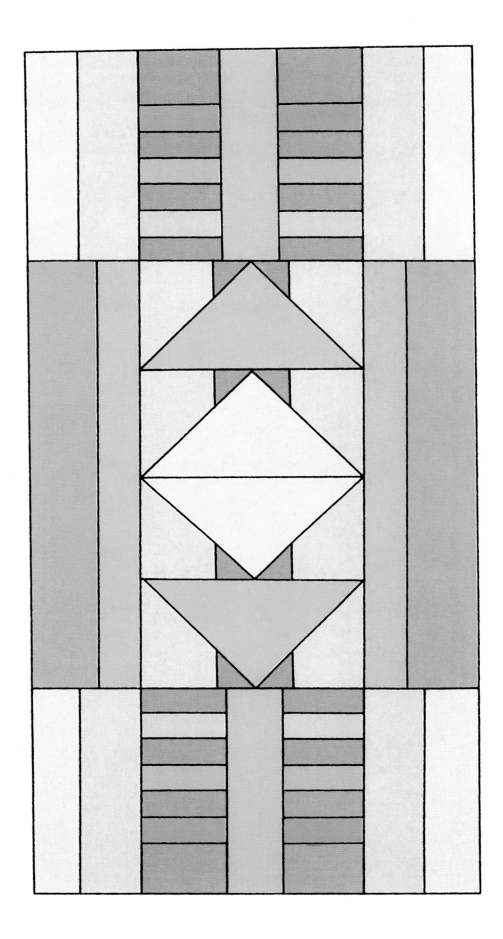

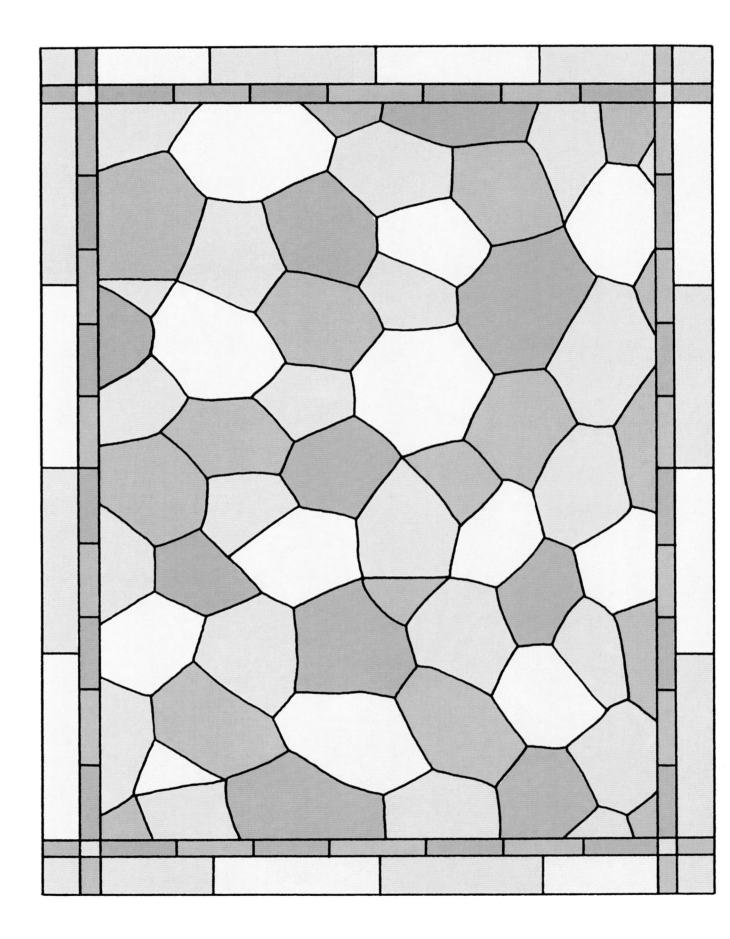

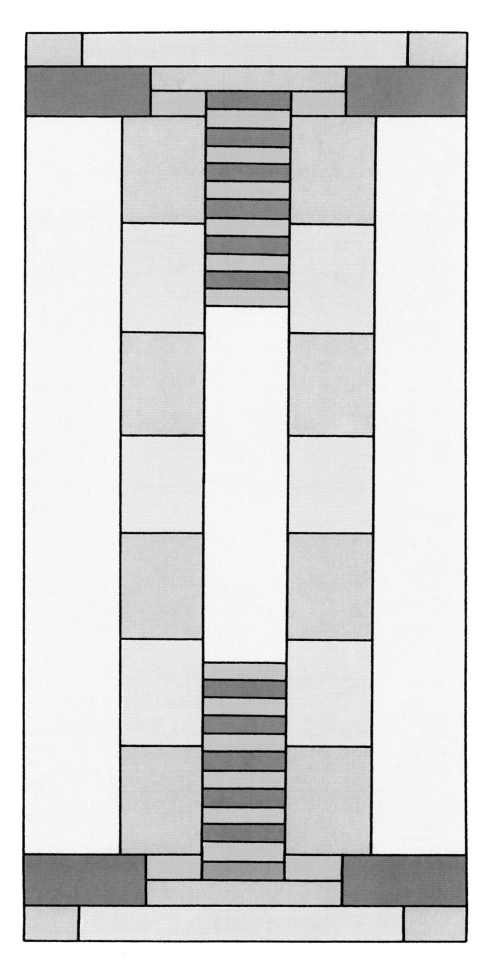

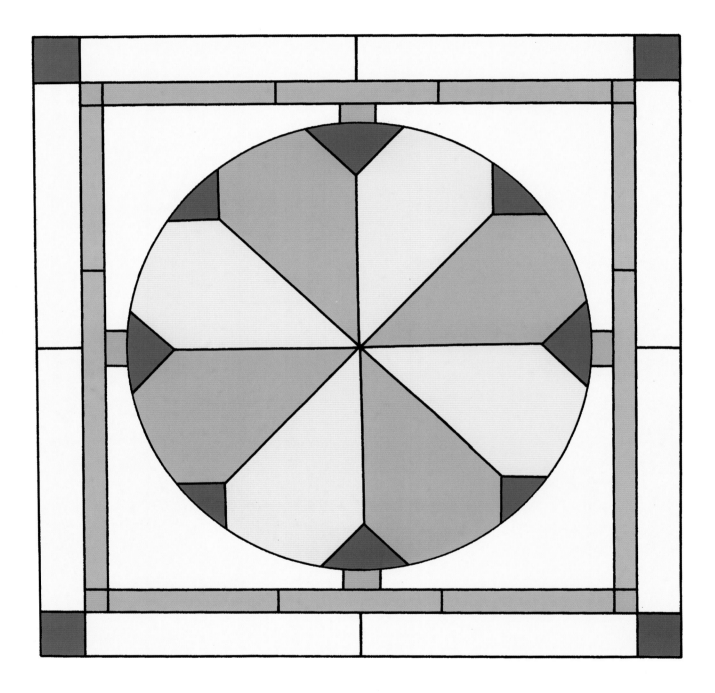

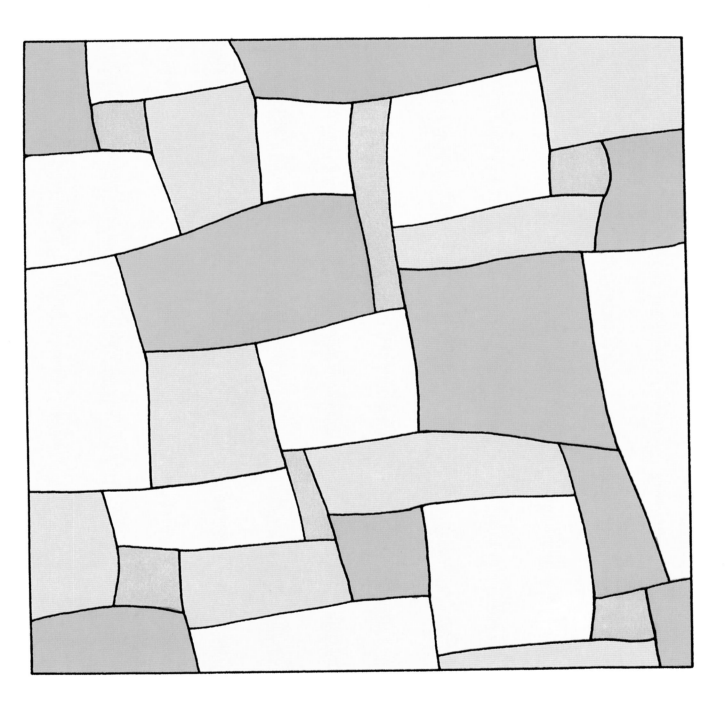

188

189

190

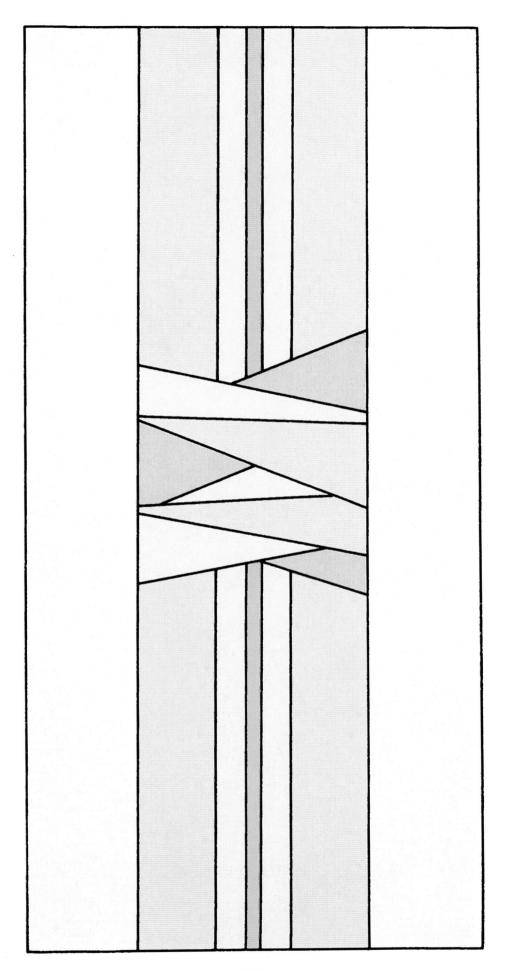